Deeper Study Guide

DEEPER

Study Guide

Real Change for Real Sinners

DANE C. ORTLUND

:: CROSSWAY®

WHEATON, ILLINOIS

Deeper Study Guide: Real Change for Real Sinners

Copyright © 2023 by Dane C. Ortlund

Published by Crossway
           1300 Crescent Street
           Wheaton, Illinois 60187

Cover design: Jordan Singer

Cover image: Museum Purchase, Gallery Fund / Bridgeman Images

First printing 2023

Printed in the United States of America

Trade paperback ISBN: 978-1-4335-9088-7

Crossway is a publishing ministry of Good News Publishers.

BP		32	31	30	29	28	27	26	25	24	23
15	14	13	12	11	10	9	8	7	6	5	4	3	2	1

Contents

Introduction

*We are complicated sinners. Sometimes we take two steps
forward and three steps back. We need time. Be patient
with yourself. A sense of urgency, yes; but not a sense
of hurry. Overnight transformations are the exception,
not the norm. Slow change is still real change.*

DANE C. ORTLUND

EVERY SINCERE CHRISTIAN longs to grow in godliness. We ache to
be more deeply conformed to the beauty of holiness that we know is
our ultimate destiny.

But growth in the Christian life is often infuriatingly elusive. That
is why pastor and author Dane Ortlund wrote the book *Deeper: Real
Change for Real Sinners.* In it he takes readers into the deep structures
of the teaching of the New Testament, offering gentle coaching to
weary Christians as they seek to cultivate holiness of life.

The reason for this *Deeper Study Guide* is to build a bridge between
Deeper and your actual life. This study guide is intended to help you
activate the truths of *Deeper* in a way that nurtures heart change and
the growth in grace that comes with it.

This study guide has been designed for various kinds of use. It
can be used in individual study, as you read through *Deeper*. It can

equally be used in a small group context or a class at your local church in conjunction with other Christians reading *Deeper* together. The study guide has been laid out in parallel with *Deeper*, with nine lessons. Each one follows the content of a chapter in *Deeper*, providing ten questions per lesson for reflection and discussion.

May this study guide and the truths it explores bring you face to face with the Savior, the Lord Jesus Christ, and your union with him, nurturing fresh grace and glory in your heart and life.

LESSON I

Jesus

1. Would you say that before reading chapter 1, you had a do-
    mesticated view of Jesus? Is your view of Jesus the same after
    reading this chapter? If not, why not?

    ....

    ....

    ....

    ....

2. What do you make of the idea that there are "regions" to the
    real Christ (in light of the Christopher Columbus analogy)
    that we haven't yet explored? How would you say that fits (or
    doesn't) your own walk with the Lord Jesus right now?

    ....

    ....

    ....

    ....

3. Has Christ's rule over this world been a truth fully aglow in your heart and mind? What will this truth mean for your day tomorrow as you roll out of bed? *(pp. 23–25)*

_____

_____

_____

_____

4. Is Jesus your full, sufficient, and all-encompassing Savior right now? Do you view his work in your life as *helping* you or as *saving* you, and why? *(pp. 25–27)*

_____

_____

_____

_____

5. How might your day tomorrow look different if the reality of Jesus Christ as your friend were not only *true* to you but *real* to you? *(pp. 27–29)*

_____

_____

_____

_____

6. No other human friend sticks with us the way Jesus does. What is one adversity or sin or darkness you are currently battling about which you need to know that Jesus will persevere with you *no matter what?* *(pp. 29–30)*

7. Do you ponder Christ's interceding work with any regularity? How do you find this truth consoling you in your walk with him right now? *(pp. 30–31)*

8. It is easy to lose an acute sense of the imminent return of Christ as we live in this world, which is constantly drawing our affections down to the things of earth. Are you finding your longing for his return growing stronger in any particular way as you read this section on Christ's return? *(pp. 31–32)*

9. How does the tenderness of Christ land on you at this season of your life? What does this mean to you? *(pp. 32–34)*

10. How do you respond to the C. S. Lewis quote with which the chapter concludes? Do you agree with it? Is this how you think of Jesus? *(p. 35)*

LESSON 2

Despair

1. As you began this book, which of the following views of the
    Christian life would you say was closer to your own view:
    (1) Christian growth is growth out of despair, as we become
    stronger; or (2) Christian growth is growth through despair,
    as we realize ever more deeply how weak we are?

2. How would you put Luther's quote on page 38 in your own
    words? Do you see this truth at play in your life at this time?

3. Pascal called human beings "glorious ruins." Which of those two realities—glory (made in God's image) and ruin (rebelliously sinful)—do you feel more keenly in yourself? Why do you think that is? *(p. 39)*

_____

_____

_____

_____

4. Reflect on your own understanding of your sinfulness. Would you say you have an accurate view of your own sin and guilt? *(pp. 40–41)*

_____

_____

_____

5. Do you recognize ways in which sin manifests itself in your life not only in immorality but also in morality? *(p. 41)*

_____

_____

_____

6. Do you think it is healthy or unhealthy to ponder regularly your sinfulness? Why? *(pp. 42–43)*

7. What is the standard next to which we must place ourselves in order to sense our sinfulness? Do you find yourself doing this with any regularity? *(pp. 43–44)*

8. Have you been believing the truth that God lives right there in your despair? That he is never closer to you than when you find yourself distressed and burdened and longing to be better? *(p. 45)*

9. Is "collapse" a word you associate with healthy Christian growth? Do you find yourself collapsing into the arms of God in your life right now? *(pp. 47–48)*

_____

_____

_____

_____

10. Chapter 2 closes with a reflection on repentance and faith. Jack Miller gets at the heart of repentance and faith with the quote on page 48. How does this quote help you *this week*?

_____

_____

_____

_____

Union

1. What was your understanding of union with Jesus Christ before beginning chapter 3? To what degree has this doctrine been a part of your understanding of who you are as a believer?

_____

_____

_____

_____

2. How would you put in your own words Paul's answer in Romans 6 as to why believers ought not "to continue in sin that grace may abound" (Rom. 6:1)? *(p. 52)*

_____

_____

_____

_____

3.   Consider your own theological journey as you look, beginning on page 53, at the taxonomy of ways we understand growth. Which of these four have you found yourself operating out of?

4.   How would you put in your own words the common truth embedded in 1 Corinthians 15:10, Philippians 2:12–13, and Colossians 1:29? *(p. 55)*

5.   What do you view as the core reality of your life? Has this chapter changed your answer in any way? *(pp. 56–57)*

6. What are the two basic ways the New Testament speaks of being in Christ? *(pp. 57–62)*

7. How can the truth of your union with Christ fortify you the next time you face an attractive temptation? *(pp. 60–61)*

8. Did the section with the heading "The Umbrella Doctrine" open up anything to you in your understanding of your salvation? *(pp. 62–64)*

9. What is the point of the Jonathan Edwards quote on pages 63–64? Have you thought of union with Christ like this before?

----

10. As you consider moving ahead into the next few days of your life, mindful of all that you are facing, what difference does your union with the risen Jesus Christ make?

Embrace

1. Describe God's love for you. Before reading chapter 4, how would you have related God's love to your growth?

_____

_____

_____

_____

2. "God made you so that he could love you." Do you believe that? *(p. 70)*

_____

_____

_____

_____

3. Do you pray prayers like Ephesians 3:16–19? If so, how have you seen those prayers answered? If not, why not? *(pp. 70–71)*

4. The author writes: "What's the state of your soul today, as you read this book? Consider your own inner life. Ponder Christ. Do you know the love of Christ?" In honesty before God, what is the answer to that right now? *(p. 71)*

5. Do you view Jesus as *essentially* loving toward you? How does Ephesians 3 or this chapter adjust your view of him? *(pp. 72–73)*

6. What do you think of when you hear the phrase "filled with all the fullness of God" (Eph. 3:19)? What is the meaning of the phrase, given its biblical context?

7. "At your point of deepest shame and regret, that's where Christ loves you the most." If you believe this, share or jot down a prayer to the Lord. *(p. 75)*

8. Do you see what John Owen is getting at in the quote on page 76? How does this affect your time in Scripture each day, or what you are aiming at when you go to church?

9. How do you experience divine love? What would have been your answer before picking up this book? Is your answer the same after reading this chapter? *(pp. 77–80)*

10. Consider the italicized portion of page 82. This is who Jesus is to you. This is his heart for you. As you close out your study of this chapter, let him love you all over again. Be at peace.

Acquittal

1. Does it surprise you to find a chapter on the gospel in a book on how Christians grow? What is your present understanding of the relationship between the good news of the gospel and your own growth in Christ? *(p. 85)*

2. What is justification, in your own words? What is sanctification, in your own words? *(pp. 86–90)*

3. How does the event of justification fuel the process of sanctification, according to this chapter? Have you thought of your growth in this way? How does this affect the way you view change in your life?

_____

_____

_____

_____

4. Had you ever before noticed the final item on the vice list in 2 Timothy 3:2–5? Do you see in your own life any tendency toward merely external conformity divorced from heart change? *(pp. 89–90)*

_____

_____

_____

_____

5. What is the author's point with regard to how exactly justification fuels sanctification? *(pp. 90–94)*

_____

_____

_____

_____

6. Have you ever considered a connection between justification and fear? What, according to Galatians 2, do you understand that connection to be? *(pp. 94–96)*

7. Do you see yourself in the bizarre story of the Nigerian inmate on page 97? How do you relate to this?

8. What might it look like in your own life to go through the coming week *fully justified*, not needing any further ratification or approval from any person or accomplishment? *(pp. 97–100)*

9. In what way is idolatry a nongospel form of justification? *(pp. 100–103)*

_____

_____

_____

_____

10. The chapter closes with three biographical snapshots from church history, featuring Martin Luther, C. S. Lewis, and Francis Schaeffer. Do you find yourself resonating with any one of these accounts in particular?

_____

_____

_____

_____

Honesty

1. What does your life among other Christians currently look like? Would you say you have deep and enriching relationships with other believers? Are you satisfied with the depth of friendship you currently enjoy at your local church?

2. What does it mean to be part of "the body of Christ"? What difference does that make for how you view other believers? *(pp. 111–12)*

3. What does it mean to "walk in the light" (1 John 1:7)? Is this a vital reality in your life right now? Would you say this is an area where you would like to grow? *(pp. 112–14)*

---

4. What holds you back from walking in the light with another brother or sister in the Lord?

---

5. How does Bonhoeffer's powerful statement on pages 114–15 strike you? Do you agree? Is your local church a haven for sinners in the way Bonhoeffer describes? Why or why not?

6. Do you see in yourself the "implicit dishonesty" that the author talks about? What is the way out of that? *(pp. 115–16)*

7. How would you answer a Christian who says, "I don't need to confess my sins to another person—I confess them to God"? *(pp. 116–17)*

8. Are you currently experiencing the "fellowship with one another" that 1 John 1:7 promises? If so, what got you there? If not, what do you think will get you there? *(pp. 118–20)*

9. Do you feel dirty? How does 1 John 1:7 speak to you today? *(pp. 120–22)*

---

10. What is one small step you can take over this next week or two to "collapse into flourishing" and experience fresh freedom as you walk in the light? *(p. 124)*

LESSON 7

Pain

1. What, right now, is the deepest pain in your life? If you are
    using this study guide in a group context, do not feel pres-
    sure to share, but consider where you are currently most an-
    guished. The purpose of chapter 7 is to let the Lord Jesus into
    that deep place of hurt.

2. Pain is not a sidebar to your life but the road on which all
    your life takes place. In what ways have you found this to be
    true recently? *(pp. 125–28)*

3. What is your current understanding of how pain fosters growth in Christ?

_____

_____

_____

_____

4. When someone opens up to us about a current anguish in his or her life, what should be our first response? *(p. 128)*

_____

_____

_____

_____

5. In what way is pain like having branches lopped off? *(pp. 128–29)*

_____

_____

_____

_____

6. Does the quote from C. S. Lewis's letter to a professor of surgery diagnose your own heart in any particular way? *(pp. 129–30)*

7. Consider the picture of the "internal fork in the road" that presents itself when life suddenly becomes deeply discouraging or difficult. Can you recall a time in your life when you were at such a fork in the road? What happened in your heart in that process? *(p. 132)*

8. Have any particular passages of Scripture opened up to you in a fresh way because of hardship in your life (as happened to Owen regarding Ps. 130:4)? *(pp. 132–33)*

9. How do Ecclesiastes 7:3 and Proverbs 14:13 upend what our culture tells us about sadness and joy? *(pp. 134–35)*

---

10. Is mortification a present reality in your life? What does it look like? *(pp. 135–37)*

Breathing

1. What do Bible reading and prayer currently look like in your life? Are you satisfied with your devotional life?

_____

_____

_____

_____

2. How have you found Scripture to help you grow in Christ? *(pp. 143–44)*

_____

_____

_____

_____

3. What does the author mean by speaking of the "reconstructing" aspect of Scripture? *(pp. 145–46)*

4. Do you think of the Bible as oxygen? How is this true in your life, or how do you desire it to become true? *(pp. 146–48)*

5. Our entire lives are a deconstructing of a wrong view of the Bible. The Scripture is a message of good news. Do you see ways in your own life or your own Bible reading where you are not yet believing this?

6. Of the nine approaches to reading Scripture on pages 149–50, which have you found yourself operating out of most often?

7. How is Bible reading like inhaling and prayer like exhaling? *(pp. 152–53)*

8. Why do you find yourself reluctant to pray? What in this book is helping you grow your impulse to pray?

9. Would you describe your prayer life as a discipline you occasionally move into, or as a way of living? How is chapter 8 helping you wade more deeply into the latter? *(pp. 153–55)*

---

10. How have you found the Psalms to fuel your prayer life? What is unique about the Psalms among all the books of the Bible? *(pp. 155–56)*

Supernaturalized *and* Conclusion

1. How would your life over the next twenty-four hours be different if the Holy Spirit were suddenly not a part of it? *(p. 159)*

2. What has been your working understanding of the Holy Spirit? How have you understood the unique roles of the Father, the Son, and the Spirit in your salvation? *(pp. 160–61)*

3. What does it mean to live in "the new age"? *(pp. 161–64)*

4. In terms of Lewis's "three kinds of men," where do you find yourself operating right now? *(pp. 164–67)*

5. Do you feel the weight of your spiritual impotence? Is that a bad thing or a good thing? Why? *(p. 167)*

6. In what specific way does the Holy Spirit change us, according to a text such as 1 Corinthians 2:12? *(pp. 167–69)*

7. What do you long for in your present life that will be possible only as a result of the work of the Holy Spirit?

8. The conclusion to *Deeper* opens, "The final conclusion, the deepest secret, to growing in Christ is this: Look to him." What do you hope this will look like in your life as you conclude your study of this book? *(p. 171)*

9. Do you think it is simplistic to view the Christian life as captured by the simple discipline of looking to Christ? Why or why not? Do you see how the various chapters of this book are all facets of looking to Christ? *(pp. 172–73)*

10. The book closes with an exquisite statement from the Scottish pastor Robert Murray McCheyne. As you read his words, jot down a prayer from your heart, expressing your longing for more of Christ in your life. May God bless you richly as you conclude your study of *Deeper* and what it means to grow in Christ. *(p. 174)*

Union

We fuel reformation in churches and lives.

Union Publishing invests in the next generation of leaders with theology that gives them a taste for a deeper knowledge of God. From books to our free online content, we are committed to producing excellent resources that will refresh, transform, and grow believers and their churches.

We want people everywhere to know, love, and enjoy God, glorifying him in everything they do. For this reason, we've collected hundreds of free articles, podcasts, book chapters, and video content for our free online collection. We also produce a fresh stream of written, audio, and video resources to help you to be more fully alive in the truth, goodness, and beauty of Jesus.

If you are hungry for reformational resources that will help you delight in God and grow in Christ, we'd love for you to visit us at unionpublishing.org.

unionpublishing.org

Also Available from Dane Ortlund

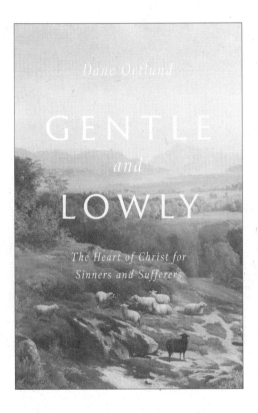

How does Jesus feel about his people amid all their sins and failures? This book takes readers into the depths of Christ's very heart—a heart of tender love drawn to sinners and sufferers.

For more information, visit **crossway.org**.